DELICIOUS LIGHT: A WEIGHT WATCHERS COOKBOOK

Healthy Recipes for Effortless weight Management

YAKS T. JONHSON

Copyright © 2024 YAKS T. JONHSON,

All rights reserved. No part of this publication may be reproduced, distributed, or transmitted in any form or by any means, Including photocopying, and recording, or other electronic or mechanical methods, without the prior written permission of the publisher, except in the case of brief quotations embodied in critical reviews and certain other noncommercial uses permitted by copyright law.

TABLE OF CONTENTS

Introduction 5
Breakfast Delights 6
    Energizing Morning Smoothies 6
    Nutritious Oatmeal Variations 9
    Wholesome Breakfast Bowls 11
Satisfying Soups and Salads 14
    Hearty Vegetable Soup 14
    Fresh Summer Salad Selections 16
    Protein-Packed Grain Salads 18
Flavorful Main Dishes 21
    Lean Protein Creations 21
    Colorful Veggie Stir-Fries 23
    Comforting Casseroles 26
Wholesome Sides and Snacks 29
    Guilt-Free Appetizers 29
    Healthy Side Dishes 32
    Smart Snacking Ideas 35
Sweet Endings 38
    Decadent Desserts Without the Guilt 38
    Fruit-Filled Treats 41
    Light and Luscious Puddings 44
Bonus: Meal Planning Tips 48
    Weekly Meal Plans 48

Grocery Shopping Made Easy 50
Tips for Dining Out 55
Conclusion 58
Final Thoughts on Your Wellness Journey 58

Introduction

Welcome to *Delicious Light: A Weight Watchers Cookbook*! In this collection of recipes, we embark on a journey to discover the joy of flavorful, nutritious meals that support your weight management goals effortlessly.

Eating well shouldn't mean sacrificing taste or satisfaction. With the recipes in this cookbook, each dish has been carefully crafted to not only be delicious but also to fit seamlessly into your Weight Watchers plan. Whether you're starting your day with a refreshing smoothie, enjoying a hearty soup for lunch, or savoring a satisfying main dish for dinner, every recipe here is designed to nourish your body and tantalize your taste buds.

Throughout this cookbook, you'll find a variety of breakfasts, soups, salads, main dishes, sides, snacks, and desserts—all with the aim of making healthy eating enjoyable and sustainable. Each recipe includes Weight Watchers points to help you track your progress and stay on target.

We believe that food is more than just fuel; it's an essential part of a balanced and fulfilling life. With *Delicious Light*, we invite you to explore a world of culinary delight that supports your journey to wellness. Whether you're new to Weight Watchers or a seasoned member, these recipes offer something for everyone.

So, let's embark together on this delicious and nutritious adventure. Here's to good food, good health, and a brighter, lighter you!

This introduction sets the tone for the cookbook, emphasizing both the enjoyment and health benefits of the recipes within the context of Weight Watchers.

Breakfast Delights

Energizing Morning Smoothies

Start your day off right with a burst of flavor and nutrition! These energizing smoothie recipes are perfect for fueling your morning and keeping you satisfied until lunchtime. Packed with vitamins, minerals, and a delicious blend of fruits and vegetables, these smoothies are also mindful of your Weight Watchers points. Enjoy experimenting with different combinations and find your favorite go-to morning boost.

1. **Berry Blast Smoothie**
   - *Ingredients: Mixed berries, Greek yogurt, spinach, almond milk*
   - *Points: 4*
2. Kick-start your day with the refreshing tang of mixed berries combined with the creaminess of Greek yogurt. Spinach adds a nutrient punch without altering the flavor, making this smoothie both delicious and packed with goodness.
3. **Green Power Smoothie**
   - *Ingredients: Kale, banana, pineapple, chia seeds, coconut water*
   - *Points: 3*
4. Loaded with kale and tropical fruits, this smoothie is a powerhouse of antioxidants and vitamins. Chia seeds add a boost of omega-3s and fiber, while coconut water provides electrolytes for a refreshing start to your morning.
5. **Mango Coconut Smoothie**
   - *Ingredients: Mango, coconut milk, plain yogurt, honey*

- Points: 5
6. Transport yourself to the tropics with this creamy mango coconut smoothie. It's a sweet and satisfying treat that's sure to brighten your morning routine. The natural sweetness of mango pairs perfectly with creamy coconut milk, creating a tropical paradise in every sip.
7. **Protein-Packed Peanut Butter Banana Smoothie**
    - *Ingredients: Banana, peanut butter, protein powder, almond milk*
    - Points: 6
8. For a more substantial breakfast option, try this protein-packed smoothie. Creamy peanut butter adds richness and a dose of healthy fats, while banana and protein powder ensure you stay full and energized throughout the morning.

These energizing morning smoothies are designed to jumpstart your day with delicious flavors and nutritious ingredients, all while supporting your Weight Watchers goals. Enjoy blending and sipping your way to a healthier you!

Nutritious Oatmeal Variations

Oatmeal is a versatile and satisfying breakfast option that can be customized to suit your taste preferences and nutritional needs. These variations on traditional oatmeal are not only delicious but also packed with nutrients to keep you fueled and satisfied all morning long. Each recipe includes Weight Watchers points to help you stay on track with your goals.

1. **Apple Cinnamon Oatmeal**
    - *Ingredients: Rolled oats, apples, cinnamon, almond milk*
    - *Points: 4*
2. Start your day with the comforting flavors of apple and cinnamon. This oatmeal is cooked to creamy perfection with diced apples and a sprinkle of warming cinnamon, creating a wholesome and satisfying breakfast.
3. **Berry Almond Overnight Oats**
    - *Ingredients: Rolled oats, mixed berries, almond butter, almond milk*
    - *Points: 5*
4. Prepare your breakfast the night before with these easy overnight oats. Mixed berries add a burst of sweetness and antioxidants, while almond butter provides a creamy texture and

a boost of healthy fats. Simply mix the ingredients and refrigerate overnight for a convenient grab-and-go option in the morning.
5. **Banana Nut Oatmeal**
    - *Ingredients: Rolled oats, banana, walnuts, honey, milk*
    - *Points: 6*
6. Bananas and walnuts add a delightful crunch and natural sweetness to this hearty oatmeal. Drizzle with a touch of honey for extra flavor, and enjoy a satisfying breakfast that's rich in fiber and essential nutrients.
7. **Pumpkin Spice Oatmeal**
    - *Ingredients: Rolled oats, pumpkin puree, maple syrup, pumpkin pie spice, milk*
    - *Points: 5*
8. Embrace the flavors of fall with this comforting pumpkin spice oatmeal. Pumpkin puree and warm spices like cinnamon, nutmeg, and cloves create a cozy breakfast that's both nutritious and indulgent. Perfect for chilly mornings or anytime you crave a taste of autumn.

These nutritious oatmeal variations offer a delicious and satisfying way to start your day while supporting your Weight Watchers journey. Whether you prefer fruity, nutty, or spicy flavors, there's a recipe here to suit every palate and keep you on track with your health goals. Enjoy exploring these wholesome breakfast options!

Wholesome Breakfast Bowls

These wholesome breakfast bowls are a delightful way to kick-start your day with a nutritious and satisfying meal. Whether you prefer sweet or savory flavors, these recipes are packed with wholesome ingredients to keep you energized and focused until lunchtime. Each bowl is designed with Weight Watchers points in mind to help you stay on track with your wellness goals.

1. **Greek Yogurt and Berry Bowl**
    - *Ingredients: Greek yogurt, mixed berries, granola, honey*
    - *Points: 5*
2. Creamy Greek yogurt layered with fresh mixed berries, crunchy granola, and a drizzle of honey creates a balanced and delicious

breakfast bowl. It's rich in protein, vitamins, and antioxidants to fuel your morning.

3. **Avocado and Egg Breakfast Bowl**
    - *Ingredients: Quinoa, avocado, poached egg, cherry tomatoes, spinach*
    - *Points: 6*
4. This savory breakfast bowl features nutrient-dense quinoa topped with creamy avocado slices, a perfectly poached egg, juicy cherry tomatoes, and fresh spinach. It's a satisfying combination of flavors and textures that will keep you satisfied and focused throughout the morning.
5. **Chia Seed Pudding Bowl**
    - *Ingredients: Chia seeds, almond milk, vanilla extract, fresh fruit, nuts*
    - *Points: 4*
6. Indulge in a nutritious and delicious chia seed pudding bowl. Chia seeds soaked in almond milk and flavored with vanilla extract create a creamy base that's topped with fresh fruits and crunchy nuts. It's a refreshing and filling option for breakfast or as a mid-morning snack.
7. **Savory Breakfast Quinoa Bowl**

- Ingredients: Quinoa, sautéed spinach, roasted sweet potatoes, chickpeas, tahini dressing
- Points: 7
8. This hearty and savory quinoa bowl is packed with protein and fiber. Sautéed spinach, roasted sweet potatoes, and chickpeas are combined with quinoa and drizzled with a creamy tahini dressing for a satisfying and nutritious breakfast option that will keep you full and satisfied.

These wholesome breakfast bowls are designed to nourish your body and support your Weight Watchers journey with flavorful and nutrient-packed ingredients. Enjoy these delicious combinations to start your day on a healthy and delicious note!

Satisfying Soups and Salads

Hearty Vegetable Soup

Warm up with a comforting bowl of hearty vegetable soup. Packed with nutrient-rich vegetables and flavorful seasonings, this soup is not only satisfying but also low in Weight Watchers points. It's perfect for lunch or dinner, and leftovers can be enjoyed throughout the week.

Ingredients:

- 1 tablespoon olive oil
- 1 onion, diced
- 2 carrots, sliced
- 2 celery stalks, sliced
- 1 bell pepper, diced
- 2 cloves garlic, minced
- 1 zucchini, diced
- 1 cup green beans, chopped
- 1 can (15 oz) diced tomatoes
- 6 cups vegetable broth
- 1 teaspoon dried thyme
- 1 teaspoon dried oregano
- Salt and pepper to taste
- Fresh parsley, chopped (for garnish)

Instructions:

1. In a large pot or Dutch oven, heat olive oil over medium heat. Add diced onion, carrots, and celery. Sauté until vegetables begin to soften, about 5-7 minutes.
2. Add bell pepper, garlic, zucchini, and green beans to the pot. Cook for another 5 minutes, stirring occasionally, until vegetables are tender.
3. Stir in diced tomatoes (with their juices) and vegetable broth. Add dried thyme, dried oregano, salt, and pepper. Bring the soup to a boil, then reduce heat and let it simmer uncovered for 20-25 minutes, or until vegetables are tender and flavors are well combined.
4. Taste and adjust seasoning if needed. If you prefer a thicker soup, you can blend a portion of the soup with an immersion blender or transfer a portion to a blender and blend until smooth, then return it to the pot.
5. Serve hot, garnished with fresh chopped parsley. Enjoy this hearty vegetable soup as a wholesome and satisfying meal!

Points per serving: 3 points (Points may vary depending on specific ingredients and serving size, adjust accordingly)

This hearty vegetable soup is not only delicious but also packed with nutrients and perfect for anyone following the Weight Watchers plan. Enjoy its comforting flavors and the satisfaction of a warm, homemade meal!

Fresh Summer Salad Selections

Enjoy the vibrant flavors of summer with these refreshing salad recipes. Packed with fresh seasonal ingredients and light dressings, these salads are perfect for hot days and make a nutritious addition to any meal. Each salad is designed with Weight Watchers points to help you stay on track with your wellness goals.

1. **Strawberry Spinach Salad**
    - *Ingredients: Baby spinach, strawberries, goat cheese, almonds, balsamic vinaigrette*
    - *Points: 4*
2. Combine baby spinach with juicy strawberries, creamy goat cheese, crunchy almonds, and a drizzle of tangy balsamic

vinaigrette. This salad is bursting with flavors and textures that scream summer.
3. **Caprese Salad**
    - *Ingredients: Fresh tomatoes, fresh mozzarella, basil leaves, balsamic glaze*
    - *Points: 5*
4. Celebrate the simplicity of summer with this classic Caprese salad. Slices of ripe tomatoes and creamy fresh mozzarella are layered with fresh basil leaves and drizzled with sweet balsamic glaze. It's a refreshing and elegant salad that highlights the best of seasonal produce.
5. **Quinoa and Chickpea Salad**
    - *Ingredients: Quinoa, chickpeas, cherry tomatoes, cucumber, red onion, feta cheese, lemon vinaigrette*
    - *Points: 6*
6. This protein-packed salad combines fluffy quinoa with hearty chickpeas, juicy cherry tomatoes, crisp cucumber, tangy red onion, and salty feta cheese. Tossed in a zesty lemon vinaigrette, it's a filling and nutritious option for a summer lunch or dinner.
7. **Watermelon Feta Salad**

- Ingredients: Watermelon, feta cheese, fresh mint, arugula, balsamic reduction
    - Points: 3
8. Enjoy a refreshing twist with this watermelon feta salad. Sweet watermelon cubes are paired with creamy feta cheese, fresh mint leaves, and peppery arugula. Drizzle with a balsamic reduction for a sweet and savory salad that's perfect for a summer barbecue or picnic.

These fresh summer salad selections are designed to showcase the vibrant flavors and abundance of seasonal produce while supporting your Weight Watchers journey. Enjoy these light and nutritious salads as part of your summer meals!

Protein-Packed Grain Salads

These hearty grain salads are packed with protein and wholesome ingredients to keep you satisfied and energized. Perfect for lunch or a light dinner, these salads are not only nutritious but also delicious with Weight Watchers points provided to help you manage your goals.

1. **Quinoa and Black Bean Salad**
     - *Ingredients: Quinoa, black beans, corn kernels, bell peppers, cilantro, lime vinaigrette*
     - *Points: 5*
2. Combine fluffy quinoa with hearty black beans, sweet corn kernels, colorful bell peppers, and fresh cilantro. Tossed in a zesty lime vinaigrette, this salad is a flavorful and satisfying meal that's packed with plant-based protein.
3. **Mediterranean Couscous Salad**
     - *Ingredients: Couscous, chickpeas, cherry tomatoes, cucumber, red onion, Kalamata olives, feta cheese, lemon herb dressing*
     - *Points: 6*
4. This Mediterranean-inspired salad features fluffy couscous tossed with protein-rich chickpeas, juicy cherry tomatoes, crisp cucumber, tangy red onion, briny Kalamata olives, and salty feta cheese. Drizzled with a refreshing lemon herb dressing, it's a filling and flavorful option for any occasion.
5. **Farro and Chicken Salad**

- *Ingredients: Farro, grilled chicken breast, roasted vegetables (e.g., bell peppers, zucchini), spinach, lemon tahini dressing*
- *Points: 7*

6. Enjoy a satisfying blend of chewy farro, tender grilled chicken breast, roasted vegetables, and fresh spinach in this hearty salad. Tossed in a creamy lemon tahini dressing, it's a protein-packed meal that's both nutritious and delicious.
7. **Wild Rice and Edamame Salad**
    - *Ingredients: Wild rice, edamame, bell peppers, carrots, green onions, sesame seeds, soy ginger dressing*
    - *Points: 6*
8. This vibrant salad combines nutty wild rice with protein-rich edamame, crunchy bell peppers, sweet carrots, and aromatic green onions. Tossed in a flavorful soy ginger dressing and garnished with sesame seeds, it's a nutritious and satisfying option that's perfect for lunch or dinner.

These protein-packed grain salads are designed to provide a delicious and filling meal while supporting your Weight Watchers goals. Enjoy the variety of flavors and textures in these nutritious salads!

Flavorful Main Dishes

Lean Protein Creations

These recipes focus on lean proteins paired with flavorful ingredients to create delicious and satisfying meals. Each dish is designed to be low in Weight Watchers points while providing essential nutrients and satisfying your hunger.

1. **Grilled Lemon Herb Chicken**
    - *Ingredients: Chicken breasts, lemon juice, garlic, herbs (such as rosemary and thyme), olive oil*
    - *Points: 4*
2. Marinate chicken breasts in a mixture of lemon juice, garlic, and herbs, then grill to perfection. This lean and flavorful dish pairs well with a variety of sides or can be sliced and added to salads or wraps for a satisfying meal.
3. **Baked Salmon with Dill Yogurt Sauce**

- *Ingredients: Salmon fillets, plain Greek yogurt, fresh dill, lemon zest, garlic*
- *Points: 5*

4. Bake salmon fillets until tender and flaky, then top with a creamy dill yogurt sauce made with Greek yogurt, fresh dill, lemon zest, and garlic. This protein-packed dish is rich in omega-3 fatty acids and bursting with fresh flavors.
5. **Turkey and Quinoa Stuffed Bell Peppers**
   - *Ingredients: Bell peppers, ground turkey, quinoa, onion, garlic, tomatoes, spinach*
   - *Points: 6*
6. Stuff bell peppers with a savory mixture of lean ground turkey, cooked quinoa, onions, garlic, diced tomatoes, and spinach. Bake until the peppers are tender and the filling is cooked through for a nutritious and satisfying meal.
7. **Tofu Stir-Fry with Vegetables**
   - *Ingredients: Extra-firm tofu, mixed vegetables (such as bell peppers, broccoli, snap peas), soy sauce, ginger, garlic*
   - *Points: 4*

8. Sauté extra-firm tofu with a colorful array of mixed vegetables in a flavorful sauce made with soy sauce, ginger, and garlic. This stir-fry is packed with plant-based protein and vibrant flavors, perfect for a quick and nutritious weeknight dinner.

These lean protein creations are designed to provide delicious and nutritious meals while supporting your Weight Watchers journey. Enjoy the variety of flavors and ingredients in these satisfying dishes!

Colorful Veggie Stir-Fries

Stir-fries are not only quick and easy to prepare but also a fantastic way to incorporate a variety of colorful vegetables into your meals. These recipes are bursting with flavor, packed with nutrients, and designed to be light on Weight Watchers points.

1. **Asian Garlic Ginger Stir-Fry**
    - *Ingredients: Mixed bell peppers (red, yellow, green), broccoli florets, snap*

> peas, carrots, garlic, ginger, soy sauce
> - Points: 4

2. Heat a wok or large skillet over medium-high heat and add a splash of olive oil. Add minced garlic and grated ginger, and cook for 30 seconds until fragrant. Add sliced mixed bell peppers, broccoli florets, snap peas, and julienned carrots. Stir-fry for about 5-7 minutes until the vegetables are tender-crisp. Drizzle with soy sauce and toss well to combine. Serve hot, garnished with sesame seeds and chopped green onions if desired.
3. **Spicy Thai Basil Vegetable Stir-Fry**
   > - *Ingredients: Mixed bell peppers (red, yellow, green), zucchini, mushrooms, Thai basil leaves, chili peppers, garlic, fish sauce, lime juice*
   > - Points: 5
4. In a large skillet or wok, heat vegetable oil over medium-high heat. Add minced garlic and sliced chili peppers (adjust amount to taste) and cook for about 30 seconds. Add sliced mixed bell peppers, zucchini, and mushrooms. Stir-fry for 5-7 minutes until vegetables are tender. Stir in Thai basil leaves, fish sauce, and a squeeze of lime

juice. Cook for another minute, then serve hot over steamed rice or quinoa.
5. **Teriyaki Tofu and Vegetable Stir-Fry**
    - *Ingredients: Extra-firm tofu, broccoli florets, bell peppers (any color), snow peas, teriyaki sauce*
    - *Points: 6*
6. Press extra-firm tofu to remove excess moisture, then cut into cubes. Heat sesame oil in a large skillet or wok over medium-high heat. Add tofu cubes and cook until golden and crispy on all sides. Remove tofu from skillet and set aside. In the same skillet, add broccoli florets, sliced bell peppers, and snow peas. Stir-fry for 5-7 minutes until vegetables are tender-crisp. Return tofu to the skillet and add teriyaki sauce. Cook for another 2-3 minutes until heated through. Serve hot, garnished with sesame seeds and chopped green onions.
7. **Mediterranean Vegetable Stir-Fry**
    - *Ingredients: Eggplant, zucchini, cherry tomatoes, red onion, garlic, Italian seasoning, olive oil*
    - *Points: 4*
8. Heat olive oil in a large skillet over medium heat. Add diced eggplant, sliced zucchini, halved cherry tomatoes, and thinly sliced red

onion. Cook, stirring occasionally, for 8-10 minutes until vegetables are tender and slightly caramelized. Stir in minced garlic and Italian seasoning, and cook for another minute. Season with salt and pepper to taste. Serve hot, garnished with fresh basil leaves and a drizzle of balsamic glaze if desired.

These colorful veggie stir-fries offer a delicious and nutritious way to enjoy a variety of vegetables while keeping your meals light and satisfying. Enjoy experimenting with different flavors and ingredients to create your favorite stir-fry combinations!

Comforting Casseroles

Casseroles are hearty, comforting dishes that are perfect for family meals or gatherings. These recipes are designed to be flavorful, satisfying, and mindful of Weight Watchers points.

1. **Chicken and Broccoli Quinoa Casserole**
    - *Ingredients: Cooked quinoa, chicken breast, broccoli florets, low-fat*

       - *shredded cheddar cheese, Greek yogurt, garlic powder, salt, pepper*
       - Points: 7
   2. Preheat the oven to 375°F (190°C). In a large bowl, mix together cooked quinoa, diced cooked chicken breast, steamed broccoli florets, low-fat shredded cheddar cheese, Greek yogurt, garlic powder, salt, and pepper. Transfer the mixture to a baking dish sprayed with cooking spray. Top with a sprinkle of additional cheese if desired. Bake for 25-30 minutes until bubbly and golden brown on top. Let cool slightly before serving.
   3. **Vegetarian Enchilada Quinoa Casserole**
       - *Ingredients: Cooked quinoa, black beans, corn kernels, bell peppers, enchilada sauce, shredded Monterey Jack cheese, cilantro*
       - Points: 6
   4. Preheat the oven to 375°F (190°C). In a large bowl, combine cooked quinoa, drained and rinsed black beans, thawed corn kernels, diced bell peppers, and enchilada sauce. Transfer the mixture to a baking dish sprayed with cooking spray. Top with shredded Monterey Jack cheese. Cover with foil and bake for 20 minutes. Remove foil

and bake for an additional 10 minutes until cheese is melted and bubbly. Garnish with fresh chopped cilantro before serving.
5. **Tuna Noodle Casserole**
    - *Ingredients: Whole wheat egg noodles, canned tuna in water, frozen peas, low-fat cream of mushroom soup, low-fat shredded cheddar cheese, breadcrumbs*
    - *Points: 8*
6. Preheat the oven to 350°F (175°C). Cook whole wheat egg noodles according to package instructions. In a large bowl, combine cooked noodles, drained canned tuna, thawed frozen peas, low-fat cream of mushroom soup, and half of the shredded cheddar cheese. Transfer the mixture to a baking dish sprayed with cooking spray. Top with remaining shredded cheddar cheese and sprinkle breadcrumbs over the top. Bake for 25-30 minutes until bubbly and golden brown on top.
7. **Sweet Potato and Black Bean Enchilada Casserole**
    - *Ingredients: Sweet potatoes, black beans, corn tortillas, enchilada sauce, shredded Mexican blend cheese, avocado, cilantro*

- *Points: 7*
8. Preheat the oven to 375°F (190°C). Peel and dice sweet potatoes, then steam until tender. In a large baking dish, layer corn tortillas, steamed sweet potatoes, drained and rinsed black beans, and enchilada sauce. Repeat layers, ending with a layer of enchilada sauce on top. Sprinkle shredded Mexican blend cheese over the top. Cover with foil and bake for 30 minutes. Remove foil and bake for an additional 10 minutes until cheese is melted and bubbly. Serve with sliced avocado and fresh chopped cilantro.

These comforting casserole recipes are perfect for cozy family dinners or gatherings with friends. They're packed with flavor and wholesome ingredients while being mindful of your Weight Watchers points. Enjoy these delicious meals that bring warmth and satisfaction to the table!

Wholesome Sides and Snacks

Guilt-Free Appetizers

These appetizers are light, flavorful, and perfect for entertaining or enjoying as a snack. They're designed to be satisfying while keeping your Weight Watchers points in check.

1. **Zucchini Fritters**
    - *Ingredients: Zucchini, whole wheat flour, Parmesan cheese, eggs, garlic powder, salt, pepper, cooking spray*
    - *Points: 3 per serving*
2. Grate zucchini and squeeze out excess moisture using a clean kitchen towel. In a bowl, combine grated zucchini, whole wheat flour, grated Parmesan cheese, beaten eggs, garlic powder, salt, and pepper. Mix until well combined. Heat a non-stick skillet over medium heat and spray with cooking spray. Drop spoonfuls of the zucchini mixture onto the skillet and flatten slightly with a spatula. Cook for 3-4 minutes per side until golden brown and cooked through. Serve hot

with a dollop of Greek yogurt or a squeeze of lemon juice.

3. **Caprese Skewers**
    - *Ingredients: Cherry tomatoes, fresh mozzarella balls (bocconcini), basil leaves, balsamic glaze*
    - *Points: 2 per skewer*
4. Assemble cherry tomatoes, fresh mozzarella balls (bocconcini), and fresh basil leaves onto skewers. Drizzle with balsamic glaze just before serving. These bite-sized skewers are a perfect combination of flavors and make a colorful and light appetizer.
5. **Cucumber Avocado Rolls**
    - *Ingredients: Cucumber, avocado, smoked salmon (optional), Greek yogurt, dill, lemon zest*
    - *Points: 4 per serving*
6. Using a mandoline or vegetable peeler, slice cucumber lengthwise into thin strips. Spread a thin layer of mashed avocado onto each cucumber strip. Top with a small piece of smoked salmon if desired. Roll up the cucumber strips and secure with toothpicks. Mix Greek yogurt with chopped dill and a pinch of lemon zest for dipping.
7. **Stuffed Mini Bell Peppers**

- Ingredients: Mini bell peppers, low-fat cream cheese, cherry tomatoes, cucumber, fresh herbs (such as parsley or chives), salt, pepper
- Points: 3 per serving

8. Cut mini bell peppers in half lengthwise and remove seeds. In a bowl, mix low-fat cream cheese with finely chopped cherry tomatoes, diced cucumber, and fresh herbs. Season with salt and pepper to taste. Fill each mini bell pepper half with the cream cheese mixture. Arrange on a serving platter and garnish with additional fresh herbs before serving.

These guilt-free appetizer recipes are perfect for any occasion, from casual gatherings to formal parties. They're light, flavorful, and designed to satisfy your appetite without compromising your health goals. Enjoy these delicious bites with friends and family!

Healthy Side Dishes

These side dishes are nutritious, flavorful, and perfect for complementing a variety of main courses. They're designed to be light, satisfying, and mindful of Weight Watchers points.

1. **Roasted Brussels Sprouts with Balsamic Glaze**
    - *Ingredients: Brussels sprouts, olive oil, balsamic glaze, salt, pepper*
    - *Points: 3 per serving*
2. Preheat the oven to 400°F (200°C). Trim and halve Brussels sprouts, then toss with olive oil, salt, and pepper on a baking sheet. Roast for 20-25 minutes until Brussels sprouts are tender and lightly caramelized. Drizzle with balsamic glaze before serving.
3. **Quinoa and Vegetable Stuffed Peppers**
    - *Ingredients: Bell peppers, cooked quinoa, mixed vegetables (such as corn, peas, carrots), black beans, salsa, shredded cheese (optional), cilantro*
    - *Points: 5 per serving*
4. Preheat the oven to 375°F (190°C). Cut tops off bell peppers and remove seeds. In a bowl, mix cooked quinoa with mixed

vegetables, drained and rinsed black beans, and salsa. Spoon the quinoa mixture into bell peppers and place in a baking dish sprayed with cooking spray. Top with shredded cheese if desired. Cover with foil and bake for 30 minutes. Remove foil and bake for an additional 10 minutes until peppers are tender and filling is heated through. Garnish with fresh cilantro before serving.

5. **Cauliflower Fried Rice**
    - *Ingredients: Cauliflower rice, mixed vegetables (such as peas, carrots, bell peppers), scrambled eggs, soy sauce, sesame oil, green onions*
    - *Points: 4 per serving*
6. In a large skillet or wok, heat sesame oil over medium heat. Add mixed vegetables and sauté until tender. Push vegetables to the side and scramble eggs in the skillet. Add cauliflower rice and soy sauce, stirring to combine. Cook for 5-7 minutes until cauliflower rice is tender and heated through. Garnish with chopped green onions before serving.
7. **Greek Cucumber Salad**
    - *Ingredients: English cucumber, cherry tomatoes, red onion, Kalamata olives,*

feta cheese, olive oil, red wine vinegar, oregano, salt, pepper
- *Points: 3 per serving*
8. Slice English cucumber into rounds and halve cherry tomatoes. Thinly slice red onion and halve Kalamata olives. In a large bowl, toss cucumber, cherry tomatoes, red onion, Kalamata olives, and crumbled feta cheese. Drizzle with olive oil and red wine vinegar. Season with dried oregano, salt, and pepper to taste. Serve chilled or at room temperature.

These healthy side dishes are perfect for enhancing any meal with nutritious ingredients and delicious flavors. Whether you're serving them with grilled proteins, roasted dishes, or as part of a vegetarian spread, they're sure to be a hit at your table while supporting your health and wellness goals. Enjoy these wholesome sides!

Smart Snacking Ideas

Certainly! Here are some smart snacking ideas from the cookbook that are both satisfying and mindful of your health goals:

Smart Snacking Ideas

These snacks are designed to be nutritious, satisfying, and perfect for curbing cravings between meals. They're light on Weight Watchers points and packed with flavor.

1. **Greek Yogurt with Fresh Berries**
   - *Ingredients: Plain Greek yogurt, mixed berries (such as strawberries, blueberries, raspberries), honey or agave syrup*
   - *Points: 2 per serving*
2. Spoon plain Greek yogurt into a bowl and top with a mix of fresh berries. Drizzle with honey or agave syrup for a touch of sweetness. This snack is rich in protein, vitamins, and antioxidants to keep you energized.
3. **Apple Slices with Almond Butter**
   - *Ingredients: Apple, almond butter*

- *Points: 3 per serving*
4. Slice an apple and serve with a side of almond butter for dipping. The combination of crunchy apple slices and creamy almond butter provides fiber, healthy fats, and a satisfying crunch.
5. **Vegetable Crudité with Hummus**
   - *Ingredients: Baby carrots, cucumber slices, cherry tomatoes, snap peas, hummus*
   - *Points: 2 per serving*
6. Arrange a variety of colorful vegetable crudité (such as baby carrots, cucumber slices, cherry tomatoes, and snap peas) on a plate. Serve with a side of hummus for dipping. This snack is packed with fiber, vitamins, and minerals to keep you full and satisfied.
7. **Hard-Boiled Eggs with Everything Bagel Seasoning**
   - *Ingredients: Hard-boiled eggs, everything bagel seasoning*
   - *Points: 2 per serving*
8. Peel hard-boiled eggs and sprinkle with everything bagel seasoning for a savory and satisfying snack. Eggs are a great source of protein and essential nutrients, while

everything bagel seasoning adds a burst of flavor.

9. **Popcorn with Parmesan Cheese**
    - *Ingredients: Air-popped popcorn, grated Parmesan cheese, salt*
    - *Points: 3 per serving*
10. Air-pop popcorn and sprinkle with grated Parmesan cheese and a pinch of salt. This light and crunchy snack is low in calories and provides whole grains and calcium from the cheese.
11. **Tuna Salad Cucumber Bites**
    - *Ingredients: Cucumber slices, canned tuna in water, Greek yogurt, Dijon mustard, lemon juice, dill, salt, pepper*
    - *Points: 2 per serving*
12. Mix canned tuna with Greek yogurt, Dijon mustard, lemon juice, chopped dill, salt, and pepper. Spoon tuna salad onto cucumber slices for a refreshing and protein-packed snack.

These smart snacking ideas are perfect for satisfying your cravings while keeping you on track with your health and wellness goals. Enjoy these nutritious and delicious snacks throughout the day!

Sweet Endings

Decadent Desserts Without the Guilt

Certainly! Here are some decadent dessert ideas from the cookbook that are guilt-free and mindful of your health goals:

Decadent Desserts Without the Guilt

Indulge in these delicious desserts that are light on Weight Watchers points but rich in flavor and satisfaction.

1. **Greek Yogurt Berry Parfait**
    - *Ingredients: Plain Greek yogurt, mixed berries (such as strawberries, blueberries, raspberries), granola or crushed nuts, honey or agave syrup*
    - *Points: 4 per serving*

2. Layer plain Greek yogurt with mixed berries in a glass or bowl. Sprinkle granola or crushed nuts between layers for added crunch. Drizzle with honey or agave syrup for sweetness. This parfait is packed with protein, vitamins, and antioxidants.
3. **Dark Chocolate Covered Strawberries**
    - *Ingredients: Fresh strawberries, dark chocolate (70% cocoa or higher)*
    - *Points: 2 per serving*
4. Melt dark chocolate in a microwave-safe bowl in 30-second intervals, stirring until smooth. Dip fresh strawberries into the melted chocolate, coating halfway. Place on a parchment-lined tray and refrigerate until chocolate sets. Enjoy these antioxidant-rich treats guilt-free.
5. **Chia Seed Pudding**
    - *Ingredients: Chia seeds, unsweetened almond milk or coconut milk, vanilla extract, honey or maple syrup, fresh fruit for topping*
    - *Points: 5 per serving*
6. Mix chia seeds with unsweetened almond milk or coconut milk, vanilla extract, and honey or maple syrup in a bowl. Stir well and refrigerate for at least 2 hours or overnight until mixture thickens into pudding

consistency. Top with fresh fruit before serving for a satisfying and fiber-rich dessert.
7. **Baked Apples with Cinnamon**
    - *Ingredients: Apples, cinnamon, nutmeg, chopped nuts (such as walnuts or almonds), honey or agave syrup*
    - *Points: 3 per serving*
8. Core apples and place in a baking dish. Sprinkle with cinnamon and nutmeg, and top with chopped nuts. Drizzle with honey or agave syrup. Bake at 375°F (190°C) for 20-25 minutes until apples are tender and caramelized. Serve warm for a comforting and naturally sweet dessert.
9. **Frozen Banana Bites**
    - *Ingredients: Bananas, dark chocolate (70% cocoa or higher), crushed nuts or shredded coconut (optional)*
    - *Points: 3 per serving*
10. Slice bananas into rounds and place on a parchment-lined tray. Melt dark chocolate in a microwave-safe bowl in 30-second intervals, stirring until smooth. Dip banana slices halfway into the melted chocolate and sprinkle with crushed nuts or shredded coconut if desired. Freeze until chocolate sets for a refreshing and satisfying treat.

These decadent desserts without the guilt are perfect for satisfying your sweet tooth while staying on track with your health and wellness goals. Enjoy these delicious treats as a reward or as a light ending to a meal!

Fruit-Filled Treats

Certainly! Here are some delicious fruit-filled treat ideas from the cookbook:

Fruit-Filled Treats

These desserts highlight the natural sweetness and flavors of fruits, offering a refreshing and nutritious way to satisfy your sweet cravings.

1. **Mixed Berry Crisp**
    - *Ingredients: Mixed berries (such as strawberries, blueberries, raspberries), oats, whole wheat flour, honey or maple syrup, cinnamon, lemon juice*

- Points: 6 per serving
2. Preheat the oven to 350°F (175°C). In a bowl, toss mixed berries with lemon juice and a drizzle of honey or maple syrup. Transfer to a baking dish sprayed with cooking spray. In another bowl, mix oats, whole wheat flour, cinnamon, and a touch of honey or maple syrup. Sprinkle the oat mixture evenly over the berries. Bake for 30-35 minutes until the topping is golden brown and the berries are bubbly. Serve warm with a dollop of Greek yogurt or a scoop of low-fat vanilla ice cream.
3. **Stuffed Baked Apples**
   - *Ingredients: Apples, dried fruit (such as raisins or cranberries), nuts (such as almonds or walnuts), cinnamon, honey or agave syrup*
   - *Points: 4 per serving*
4. Core apples and place in a baking dish. In a bowl, mix dried fruit, chopped nuts, cinnamon, and a drizzle of honey or agave syrup. Stuff the mixture into the cored apples. Bake at 375°F (190°C) for 25-30 minutes until apples are tender and filling is heated through. Serve warm for a comforting and naturally sweet dessert.
5. **Fruit Salad with Mint Lime Dressing**

- Ingredients: Assorted fresh fruits (such as watermelon, pineapple, grapes, kiwi), fresh mint leaves, lime juice, honey or agave syrup
- Points: 3 per serving
6. Chop assorted fresh fruits into bite-sized pieces and combine in a bowl. In a small bowl, whisk together fresh lime juice, chopped mint leaves, and honey or agave syrup. Drizzle the dressing over the fruit salad and toss gently to combine. Serve chilled or at room temperature for a refreshing and light dessert or snack.
7. **Grilled Fruit Skewers**
    - Ingredients: Assorted fruits (such as pineapple chunks, peach slices, banana rounds), honey or maple syrup, cinnamon
    - Points: 2 per skewer
8. Preheat a grill or grill pan over medium-high heat. Thread assorted fruit onto skewers, alternating varieties. Brush fruit skewers with honey or maple syrup and sprinkle with cinnamon. Grill for 3-4 minutes per side until fruit is tender and lightly caramelized. Serve warm as a delightful and naturally sweet dessert.
9. **Frozen Yogurt Bark with Berries**

- *Ingredients: Greek yogurt, mixed berries (such as strawberries, blueberries, raspberries), honey or agave syrup*
- *Points: 4 per serving*
10. Line a baking sheet with parchment paper. Spread Greek yogurt evenly over the parchment paper. Sprinkle mixed berries over the yogurt and drizzle with honey or agave syrup. Freeze for 2-3 hours until firm. Break into pieces and serve as a refreshing and creamy dessert.

These fruit-filled treats are perfect for enjoying the natural sweetness of fruits while providing essential vitamins, minerals, and fiber. They're light, satisfying, and a delightful way to incorporate more fruits into your diet. Enjoy these refreshing desserts guilt-free!

Light and Luscious Puddings

Certainly! Here are some light and luscious pudding recipes from the cookbook that are delicious and mindful of your health goals:

Light and Luscious Puddings

These pudding recipes are creamy, satisfying, and perfect for a guilt-free dessert option.

1. **Chia Seed Pudding with Fresh Fruit**
   - *Ingredients: Chia seeds, unsweetened almond milk or coconut milk, vanilla extract, honey or maple syrup, mixed fresh fruit (such as berries, mango, kiwi)*
   - *Points: 5 per serving*
2. In a bowl, mix chia seeds with unsweetened almond milk or coconut milk, vanilla extract, and honey or maple syrup. Stir well and refrigerate for at least 2 hours or overnight until mixture thickens into pudding consistency. Serve chilled, topped with mixed fresh fruit for a refreshing and fiber-rich dessert.
3. **Avocado Chocolate Pudding**
   - *Ingredients: Ripe avocados, unsweetened cocoa powder, honey or agave syrup, vanilla extract, almond milk or coconut milk*
   - *Points: 6 per serving*

4. Blend ripe avocados, unsweetened cocoa powder, honey or agave syrup, vanilla extract, and a splash of almond milk or coconut milk in a food processor or blender until smooth and creamy. Adjust sweetness to taste. Chill in the refrigerator for 1-2 hours before serving. This creamy and decadent pudding is packed with healthy fats and antioxidants.
5. **Coconut Tapioca Pudding**
    - *Ingredients: Tapioca pearls, light coconut milk, honey or maple syrup, vanilla extract, shredded coconut (optional)*
    - *Points: 7 per serving*
6. Cook tapioca pearls according to package instructions using light coconut milk instead of water. Stir in honey or maple syrup and vanilla extract while cooking. Once tapioca pearls are translucent and mixture has thickened, remove from heat and let cool slightly. Serve warm or chilled, sprinkled with shredded coconut if desired. This pudding is creamy and delicately sweet with a hint of coconut flavor.
7. **Lemon Yogurt Pudding**

- Ingredients: Plain Greek yogurt, lemon zest, lemon juice, honey or agave syrup, vanilla extract
- Points: 4 per serving

8. In a bowl, mix plain Greek yogurt with lemon zest, fresh lemon juice, honey or agave syrup, and vanilla extract until smooth. Chill in the refrigerator for at least 1 hour before serving. This tangy and refreshing pudding is high in protein and perfect for citrus lovers.

9. **Rice Pudding with Cinnamon**
   - Ingredients: Arborio rice, unsweetened almond milk or coconut milk, honey or maple syrup, cinnamon, vanilla extract
   - Points: 6 per serving

10. Cook Arborio rice in unsweetened almond milk or coconut milk with a pinch of cinnamon and honey or maple syrup until rice is tender and mixture is creamy. Stir in vanilla extract towards the end of cooking. Serve warm or chilled, sprinkled with a dusting of cinnamon. This comforting rice pudding is rich and creamy without the guilt.

These light and luscious pudding recipes offer a variety of flavors and textures while being mindful of your health goals. Enjoy these creamy desserts as a satisfying end to a meal or a delightful snack!

Bonus: Meal Planning Tips

Weekly Meal Plans

Creating a weekly meal plan can be a great way to stay organized and ensure you're eating nutritious meals throughout the week. Here's a sample weekly meal plan from the "Delicious Light: A Weight Watchers Cookbook" that includes a variety of dishes for breakfast, lunch, and dinner:

Weekly Meal Plan

Monday:

- **Breakfast:** Energizing Morning Smoothie
- **Lunch:** Hearty Vegetable Soup
- **Dinner:** Colorful Veggie Stir-Fry

Tuesday:

- **Breakfast:** Nutritious Oatmeal Variations
- **Lunch:** Fresh Summer Salad Selections
- **Dinner:** Protein-Packed Grain Salads

Wednesday:

- **Breakfast:** Wholesome Breakfast Bowls
- **Lunch:** Lean Protein Creations
- **Dinner:** Mediterranean Vegetable Stir-Fry

Thursday:

- **Breakfast:** Energizing Morning Smoothie
- **Lunch:** Hearty Vegetable Soup
- **Dinner:** Protein-Packed Grain Salads

Friday:

- **Breakfast:** Nutritious Oatmeal Variations
- **Lunch:** Fresh Summer Salad Selections
- **Dinner:** Colorful Veggie Stir-Fry

Saturday:

- **Breakfast:** Wholesome Breakfast Bowls
- **Lunch:** Lean Protein Creations
- **Dinner:** Mediterranean Vegetable Stir-Fry

Sunday:

- **Breakfast:** Energizing Morning Smoothie

- **Lunch:** Hearty Vegetable Soup
- **Dinner:** Colorful Veggie Stir-Fry

Notes:

- **Snacks:** Incorporate smart snacking ideas such as Greek yogurt with berries, apple slices with almond butter, or vegetable crudité with hummus throughout the week.
- **Desserts:** Enjoy guilt-free fruit-filled treats or light and luscious puddings for dessert options.
- **Variations:** Feel free to swap out meals within the same category (e.g., swap one stir-fry recipe for another) based on your preferences and ingredient availability.

This meal plan provides a balance of flavors and nutrients while keeping portions in check with Weight Watchers points. Adjust serving sizes and ingredients as needed to fit your specific dietary needs and enjoy a week of delicious and healthy eating!

Grocery Shopping Made Easy

To make grocery shopping easier based on the weekly meal plan provided earlier, here's a simplified grocery list organized by categories. This list includes ingredients needed for breakfast, lunch, dinner, snacks, and desserts:

Grocery Shopping List

Produce:

- Mixed berries (e.g., strawberries, blueberries, raspberries)
- Apples
- Avocados
- Fresh mint leaves
- Lemons
- Limes
- Mixed fresh fruits (e.g., watermelon, pineapple, kiwi)
- Zucchini
- Broccoli florets
- Bell peppers (assorted colors)
- Cherry tomatoes
- Cucumber
- Sweet potatoes

- Cauliflower
- English cucumber
- Baby carrots
- Snap peas
- Red onion
- Garlic

Dairy and Eggs:

- Plain Greek yogurt
- Low-fat cream cheese
- Low-fat shredded cheddar cheese
- Feta cheese
- Eggs

Grains and Cereals:

- Quinoa
- Whole wheat egg noodles
- Whole wheat flour
- Rolled oats
- Arborio rice
- Popcorn kernels

Proteins:

- Chicken breast
- Canned tuna in water
- Black beans (canned)

- Tofu or tempeh (optional for vegetarian options)
- Frozen peas
- Frozen corn kernels

Pantry Staples:

- Chia seeds
- Almond butter
- Honey or agave syrup
- Maple syrup
- Olive oil
- Sesame oil
- Balsamic glaze or vinegar
- Soy sauce
- Dijon mustard
- Cinnamon
- Nutmeg
- Everything bagel seasoning
- Breadcrumbs

Frozen:

- Frozen mixed berries (if fresh not available)
- Frozen spinach (optional for smoothies)

Bakery:

- Granola or crushed nuts (for parfaits)

Miscellaneous:

- Cooking spray
- Dark chocolate (70% cocoa or higher)
- Unsweetened cocoa powder
- Dark chocolate chips (optional)
- Shredded coconut (optional)

Herbs and Spices:

- Fresh dill
- Fresh cilantro
- Fresh parsley
- Oregano (dried)
- Vanilla extract

Beverages:

- Unsweetened almond milk or coconut milk (for recipes)
- Green tea or herbal tea (optional)

Tips:

1. **Check Pantry Staples:** Before shopping, review what you already have at home to avoid unnecessary purchases.

2. **Fresh vs. Frozen:** Opt for fresh produce when possible, but keep frozen alternatives on hand for convenience and longer shelf life.
3. **Meal Preparation:** Prep ingredients like chopping vegetables or cooking grains ahead of time to streamline meal preparation during the week.
4. **Flexible Substitutions:** Feel free to substitute ingredients based on availability or dietary preferences while keeping the overall balance of nutrients in mind.

By using this grocery list, you'll have everything you need to prepare the meals from the weekly meal plan efficiently and enjoy delicious, healthy dishes throughout the week!

Tips for Dining Out

When dining out while following a healthy eating plan like Weight Watchers, it's important to make mindful choices that align with your goals. Here are some tips to help you navigate dining out:

1. **Plan Ahead:**
   - **Check the Menu:** Look up the restaurant's menu online before you go. Many restaurants now provide nutritional information, which can help you make informed choices.
   - **Choose Wisely:** Decide what you'll order in advance to avoid impulse decisions when you arrive.
2. **Focus on Balance:**
   - **Lean Proteins:** Opt for grilled, baked, or steamed proteins such as chicken, fish, or tofu. Avoid fried or breaded options.
   - **Vegetables:** Choose dishes with plenty of vegetables. Ask for steamed or grilled vegetables instead of those cooked in heavy sauces.
   - **Whole Grains:** Look for whole grain options like brown rice, quinoa, or whole wheat pasta instead of refined grains.
3. **Portion Control:**
   - **Share or Half Portions:** Consider sharing a dish with a friend or family member, or ask for a half portion to control your portions.

- Take Home Extras: If the portion sizes are large, ask for a take-home container when your meal arrives and set aside part of your meal before you start eating.
4. **Mindful Eating:**
    - **Eat Slowly:** Enjoy your meal slowly and savor each bite. This gives your body time to recognize when you're full, helping you avoid overeating.
    - **Listen to Your Body:** Stop eating when you feel satisfied, even if there is food left on your plate.
5. **Make Special Requests:**
    - **Ask for Modifications:** Don't be afraid to ask for adjustments to dishes to suit your preferences and dietary needs (e.g., dressing on the side, sauce on the side, steamed instead of fried).
6. **Beverage Choices:**
    - **Water:** Opt for water or unsweetened beverages instead of sugary drinks or alcohol, which can add unnecessary calories.
    - **Lighter Options:** If you choose alcohol, opt for light beer, wine

spritzers, or cocktails made with low-calorie mixers.
7. **Dessert Strategies:**
    - **Share Desserts:** If you want dessert, share it with others at your table to enjoy a taste without overindulging.
    - **Fruit Options:** Look for fruit-based desserts or options like sorbet which are typically lower in calories than rich cakes or pies.
8. **Stay Flexible and Enjoy:**
    - **Enjoy the Experience:** Dining out is also about enjoying the experience and socializing. Focus on making healthier choices most of the time but allow yourself flexibility to enjoy special occasions.

By following these tips, you can make dining out an enjoyable experience while staying on track with your health and weight management goals.

Conclusion

Final Thoughts on Your Wellness Journey

As you conclude your wellness journey, remember that it's a continuous process of making mindful choices that support your health and happiness. Here are some final thoughts to keep in mind:

1. **Consistency Over Perfection:** Strive for consistency in making healthy choices rather than aiming for perfection. Small, sustainable changes over time can lead to significant improvements in your overall well-being.
2. **Balance is Key:** Find a balance that works for you between nutritious eating, physical activity, rest, and mental well-being. It's about nourishing both your body and mind.
3. **Set Realistic Goals:** Set achievable goals that align with your lifestyle and values. Celebrate your progress, whether it's reaching a fitness milestone, trying new healthy recipes, or managing stress more effectively.
4. **Embrace Variety:** Keep your meals and activities varied to prevent boredom and

ensure you're getting a wide range of nutrients and experiences.
5. **Self-Compassion:** Be kind to yourself on your journey. There will be ups and downs, but each step you take towards better health is an accomplishment.
6. **Seek Support:** Surround yourself with supportive friends, family, or communities who share your goals or can encourage you along the way.
7. **Lifelong Learning:** Stay curious and continue learning about nutrition, fitness, and wellness. This knowledge empowers you to make informed choices that benefit your health.
8. **Enjoy the Process:** Remember that wellness is not just about reaching a specific goal but enjoying the journey itself. Find joy in cooking nutritious meals, exploring new physical activities, and nurturing your well-being.

By integrating these principles into your daily life, you can cultivate a sustainable approach to wellness that supports your long-term health and happiness. Celebrate your achievements, learn from challenges, and continue embracing a balanced and fulfilling lifestyle.

Printed in Great Britain
by Amazon